Contents

Some words are shown in bold, **like this**. They are explained in the glossary on page 23.

What is a triangle?

A triangle is **flat** shape with three **corners**.

You can see flat shapes but you cannot pick them up.

Finding Shapes

Triangles

Diyan Leake

www.raintreepublishers.co.uk

Visit our website to find out more information about **Raintree** books.

To order:

☎ Phone 44 (0) 1865 888112

🖹 Send a fax to 44 (0) 1865 314091

💻 Visit the Raintree Bookshop at **www.raintreepublishers.co.uk** to browse our catalogue and order online.

First published in Great Britain by Raintree,
Halley Court, Jordan Hill, Oxford OX2 8EJ,
part of Harcourt Education.
Raintree is a registered trademark of Harcourt
Education Ltd.

Editorial: Diyan Leake
Design: Joanna Hinton-Malivoire
Picture research: Maria Joannou
Production: Victoria Fitzgerald
Originated by Dot Gradations Ltd
Printed and bound in China by
South China Printing Company

10 digit ISBN 1 844 21334 X (HB)
13 digit ISBN 978 1844 21334 4 (HB)
10 09 08 07 06
10 9 8 7 6 5 4 3 2 1

10 digit ISBN 1 844 21349 8 (PB)
13 digit ISBN 978 1844 21349 8 (PB)
10 09 08 07
10 9 8 7 6 5 4 3 2 1

British Library Cataloguing in Publication Data
Leake, Diyan
561.1'5
Finding Shapes: Triangles
A full catalogue record for this book is available
from the British Library.

Acknowledgements
The publishers would like to thank the following
for permission to reproduce photographs:
Aviation Images p. 16 (M. Wagner); Corbis pp. 6
(Sandro Vannini), 7; Getty Images pp. 13
(Taxi/Eri Morita), 15 (Stone/Mitch Epstein), 18
(Botanica), 19 (Photodisc), back cover (boat,
Botanica; slide, Taxi/Eri Morita); Harcourt
Education Ltd pp. 5 (Malcolm Harris), 8
(Malcolm Harris), 9 (Tudor Photography), 10
(Malcolm Harris), 11 (Tudor Photography), 12
(Malcolm Harris), 17 (top & bottom, Tudor
Photography), 20 (Tudor Photography), 21
(Tudor Photography), 22 (Tudor Photography),
23 (pyramid, Tudor Photography; straight,
Malcolm Harris); Rex Features p. 14 (The Travel
Library)

Cover photograph reproduced with the
permission of Alamy

Every effort has been made to contact copyright
holders of any material reproduced in this book.
Any omissions will be rectified in subsequent
printings if notice is given to the publishers.

...uld like to thank
... Years Education,
...e of Education, for
...he preparation of

...book comes from

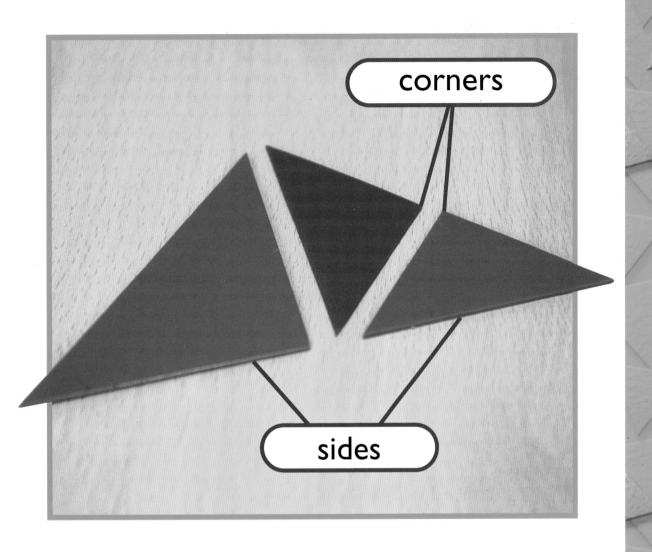

All triangles have three **sides**.

The sides are **straight**.

5

Where can I see triangles?

There are triangles all around us.

The top of a house may have a triangle shape.

The **sides** of a triangle are not always the same length.

Are there triangles at home?

We can cut some food into triangle shapes.

We can fold paper napkins into triangles.

These pieces of cheese are cut in a triangle shape.

Can I see triangles at school?

There are small triangles and big triangles at school.

These triangles are small enough to hold.

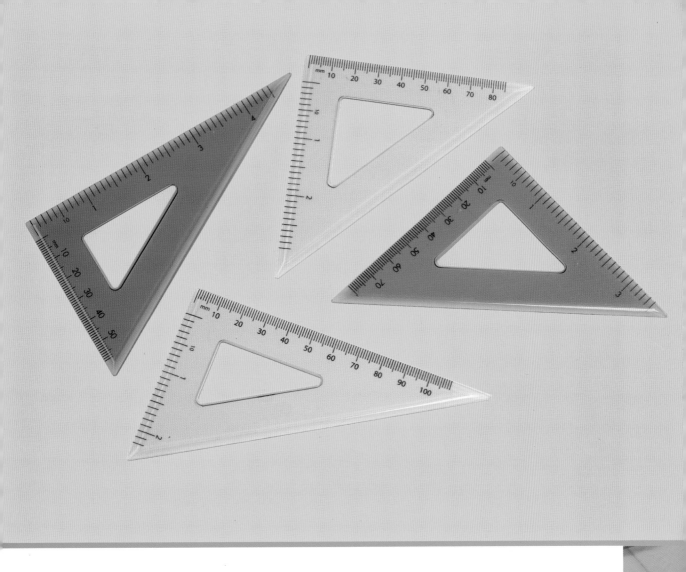

These triangles are good for
drawing **straight** lines and **corners**.
What big triangles are there
at school?

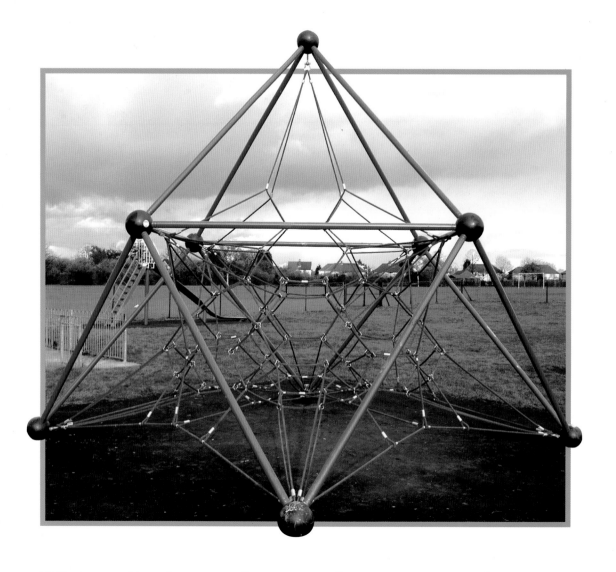

This climbing frame has triangles on it.

The net in the frame is made of red plastic rope.

The frame of a slide has a triangle.

You slide down one **side** of the triangle.

Are there triangles outside?

Parts of these tents are triangles.

People sleep in tents when they go camping.

These triangles are blowing in the wind.

They are red, white, and blue.

Do airplanes have triangles?

This airplane has triangles on its wings.

It is zooming across the sky.

You can fold paper into
an airplane.

The wings of a paper airplane
have a triangle shape.

Do boats and ships have triangles?

Some boats have sails in the shape of a triangle.

The wind fills the sails to move the boat along.

Ships may have flags of different colours on them.

Some of the flags are triangles.

Can triangles be part of other shapes?

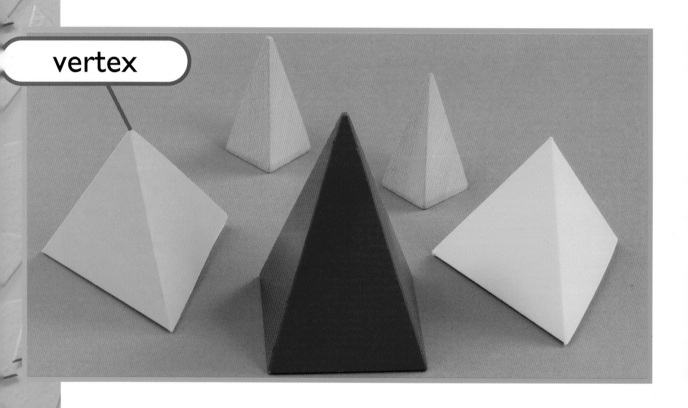

vertex

Triangles can be part of a shape called a **pyramid**.

All the triangles in a pyramid meet at one **vertex**.

The bottom of a pyramid can be a triangle.

It can be a **square**.

Can I go on a triangle walk?

Walk around the playground and see how many triangles you can find!

Glossary

 **corners**
parts of a shape where the sides come together

 **flat**
level and has no thickness to it

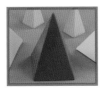 **pyramid**
shape that has triangles that all come together at one vertex

 **sides**
the outside lines that are part of a flat shape

 **square**
flat shape with four corners and four straight sides that are all the same size

 **straight**
not bent or curved

 vertex
corner of a shape

Index

Note to parents and teachers

Reading non-fiction texts for information is an important part of a child's literacy development. Readers can be encouraged to ask simple questions and then use the text to find the answers. Each chapter in this book begins with a question. Read the questions together. Look at the pictures. Talk about what the answer might be. Then read the text to find out if your predictions were correct. To develop readers' enquiry skills, encourage them to think of other questions they might ask about the topic. Discuss where you could find the answers. Assist children in using the contents page, picture glossary, and index to practise research skills and new vocabulary.